Civil War and Reconstruction in Florida

Kelly Rodgers

Consultants

Dorothy Levin, M.S.Ed., MBA
St. Lucie County Schools

Vanessa Ann Gunther, Ph.D.
Department of History
Chapman University

Cassandra Slone
Pinellas County Public Schools

Publishing Credits
Rachelle Cracchiolo, M.S.Ed., *Publisher*
Conni Medina, M.A.Ed., *Managing Editor*
Emily R. Smith, M.A.Ed., *Series Developer*
Diana Kenney, M.A.Ed., NBCT, *Content Director*
Courtney Patterson, *Multimedia Designer*

Image Credits: Cover, pp.1, 2-3, 8-9 LOC [LC-USZC2-2353]; cover, pp.1, 9, 12, 15, 16-17, 29 (top and bottom) State Archives of Florida; pp.4-5, 20-21, 21 (top) North Wind Picture Archives; p.5 LOC [rbpe.0220120b]; p.6 LOC [LC-DIG-hec-10970]; p.7 (bottom) LOC [LC-DIG-ppmsca-19483], (top) Courtesy of the Museum of Florida History; p.9 LOC [LC-DIG-stereo-1s03935]; pp.10, back cover Don Troiani/Corbis; pp.11, 23, 29 (middle) Granger, NYC; p.13 LOC [g3701s.cw011000]; pp.14-15 Washington University Department of Special Collections/Public Domain; pp.17 (top), 32 Courtesy of the Museum of Florida History, (bottom) Photo by William B. Lees, used with permission, Florida Public Archaeology Network, University of West Florida; p.18 LOC [LC-DIG-ppmsca-19204]; p.19 LOC [LC-DIG-pga-01895]; pp.21 (bottom) LOC [LC-DIG-cwpbh-00343]; pp.24-25 LOC [LC-DIG-det-4a03585]; p.25 NARA [528542]; p.28 (right) LOC [LC-DIG-ppmsca-21512], (left) LOC [LC-DIG-ppmsca-33798]; p.31 LOC [LC-DIG-hec-10970]; all other images from iStock and/or Shutterstock.

Library of Congress Cataloging-in-Publication Data

Names: Rodgers, Kelly, author.
Title: Civil War and Reconstruction in Florida / Kelly Rodgers.
Description: Huntington Beach, CA : Teacher Created Materials, [2017] |
  Includes index. | Audience: 4-6.
Identifiers: LCCN 2016014353 (print) | LCCN 2016016843 (ebook) | ISBN
  9781493835393 (pbk.) | ISBN 9781480756373 (eBook)
Subjects: LCSH: Florida--History--Civil War, 1861-1865--Juvenile literature.
  | Reconstruction (U.S. history, 1865-1877)--Florida--Juvenile literature.
Classification: LCC F316 .R645 2017 (print) | LCC F316 (ebook) | DDC
  975.9/05--dc23
LC record available at https://lccn.loc.gov/2016014353

Teacher Created Materials
5301 Oceanus Drive
Huntington Beach, CA 92649-1030
http://www.tcmpub.com
ISBN 978-1-4938-3539-3
© 2017 Teacher Created Materials, Inc.

Table of Contents

A New Way of Life	4
Leaving the Union	6
Pensacola Powder Keg	8
Civil War in Florida	10
Victory!	18
Reconstruction	20
Slowly Rebuilding	22
Rebuilding the Railroad	24
Looking to the Future	26
Author It!	28
Glossary	30
Index	31
Your Turn!	32

A New Way of Life

By the mid 1800s, cotton was king across the South. Then, an uprising began in the Southern states in late 1860. The new president, Abraham Lincoln, was against the spread of slavery. Rich **plantation** owners depended on slave labor. They were afraid Lincoln would **outlaw** it. They were willing to fight to keep their way of life. Soon, war broke out.

The people of Florida played a unique role in the war. They fought on both sides. Most sided with the other Southern states. Some supported the **Union**. Several battles were fought in Florida. And, farmers in the state supplied food to the Southern army.

Cotton is loaded onto a steamboat in Florida.

The war was long. Hundreds of thousands died. It changed the country, and it changed Florida, too. When the war was over, slavery was outlawed. The country began to rebuild. The people of Florida had to make a new way of life. Was Florida ready to move forward?

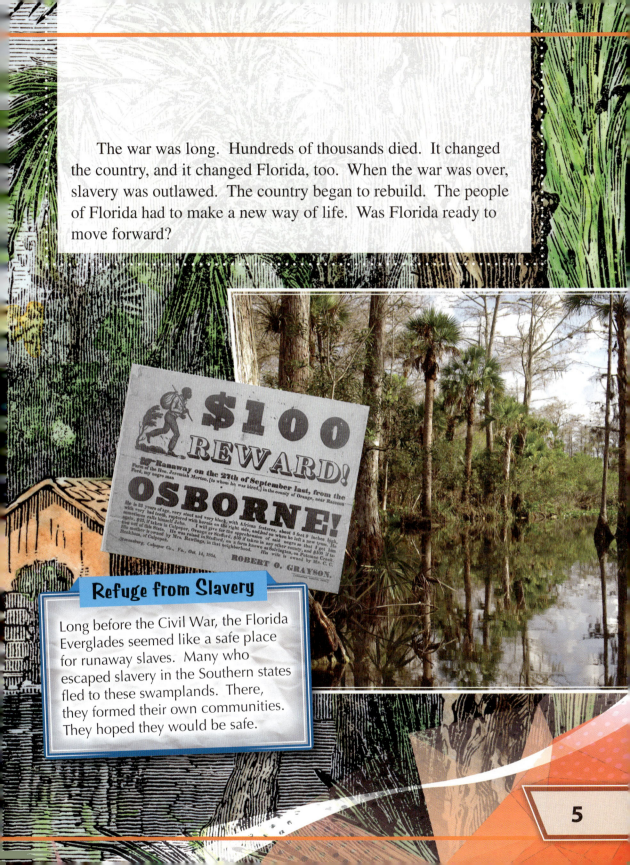

Refuge from Slavery

Long before the Civil War, the Florida Everglades seemed like a safe place for runaway slaves. Many who escaped slavery in the Southern states fled to these swamplands. There, they formed their own communities. They hoped they would be safe.

Leaving the Union

Florida was a small state before the Civil War. Only about 140,000 people lived there. This was very low compared to other states, many of which had more than a million people.

Since the state was still so rural, farming was a big part of the economy. As a result, the plantation owners had a lot of power. When Lincoln was elected President in 1860, they were afraid he would end slavery. This would greatly reduce their profits. So, the Southern states chose to **secede**, or leave, the Union.

South Carolina was the first to secede. Mississippi was next. Florida's planters decided to join them. Even though other people in the state disagreed, the planters had the most power. They had the final say.

Lincoln was worried. He was afraid the country was heading for war. Lincoln said the states could not form their own country. He said they were a part of the United States. If they left, it would be a rebellion.

Leaving Out Lincoln

No one in Florida voted for Abraham Lincoln to be president. His name was not included on the ballot. He was also left off the ballot in Alabama, Arkansas, Georgia, Louisiana, Mississippi, North Carolina, Tennessee, and Texas.

A New Flag

Helen Broward and other women of Duval County made a flag to show their support for secession. They sent it to Florida's governor as a gift. The flag has three stars to represent the first three states that left the Union. The banner reads "The Rights of the South at all Hazards."

South Carolina, Mississippi, and Florida were the first states to secede from the Union.

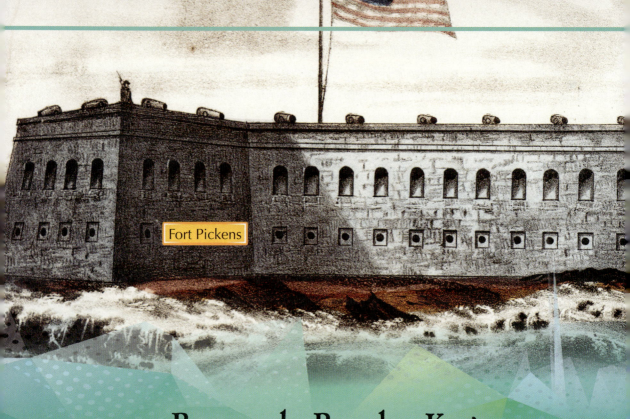

Pensacola Powder Keg

Florida seceded on January 10, 1861. By January 28, it joined the other Southern states. They had formed their own government. They called it the Confederate States of America. Although small in numbers, Florida was important in the war effort. There were many forts along its coast. Whoever controlled the forts could control Florida.

There were four forts in Pensacola Bay. The forts protected the harbor. Union troops wanted to control the forts. Union troops had already gained control of Fort Pickens on Santa Rosa Island. The **Confederates** captured the other three. They demanded that the Union troops **surrender**. But they refused. It looked like war might break out in the state. So, the leaders on both sides worked out a deal. The Southern troops promised not to attack Fort Pickens. The Union leaders promised not to send any more troops to reinforce the fort. There was an uneasy peace.

This is Fort Sumter's entrance after being attacked.

But war did break out. The first battle took place at Fort Sumter in South Carolina, in April of 1861. This was the start of the Civil War. President Lincoln fought to **reunite** the country. The Southern states fought for their way of life.

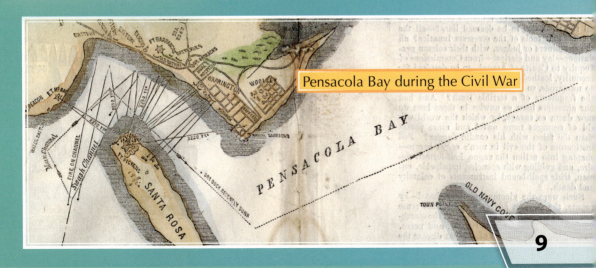

Pensacola Bay during the Civil War

Civil War in Florida

Fifteen thousand of Florida's men fought in the war. They wanted to fight for their way of life. But few battles were fought in the state. Most of the battles were fought elsewhere. The soldiers went where they were needed. People in the state found other ways to help the war effort on the home front. Florida's crops helped feed many Southern troops. Other people helped make uniforms.

Salt making, in particular, was a key part of Florida's contribution to the war effort. Salt was used to preserve food. The Union tried to block salt shipments into the South. Without it, food would spoil. There would be less food for troops. But people found other ways. They made salt by boiling seawater. Once the water evaporated, the salt was collected from the pan or kettle.

Confederate soldier uniform

Women Aid the War Effort

Women contributed to the war effort, too. Some women formed sewing circles to make uniforms for soldiers. Others worked as nurses to help the sick and wounded. Many ran family farms while their husbands were away in battle.

A slave harvests sea salt.

The Union in Florida

About 2,000 of Florida's soldiers fought for the North. They did not want to secede. Since many of them were merchants, they did not depend on slave labor. Other people did not like that men were **drafted** and forced to fight for the South. They did not want their cattle seized by the army, either. They wanted to live life as usual. In time, this disgust led them to fight for the Union.

The Union's war **strategy** was to create a **blockade** around the southern coast. A blockade is something that keeps people or goods from getting where they need to go. The blockade kept the South from moving troops, weapons, and food. The Union hoped it would cut off trade, too. The South would have less money if it could not ship cotton. Without money and supplies, soldiers would not be able to keep fighting.

That's not to say that some goods didn't make it through. **Blockade-runners** were boats that slipped through inlets to get things past Union forces. The owners of these boats made quite a bit of money bringing in supplies, such as bullets and coffee.

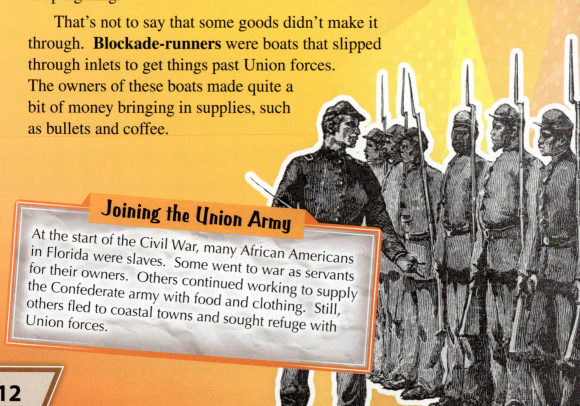

Joining the Union Army

At the start of the Civil War, many African Americans in Florida were slaves. Some went to war as servants for their owners. Others continued working to supply the Confederate army with food and clothing. Still others fled to coastal towns and sought refuge with Union forces.

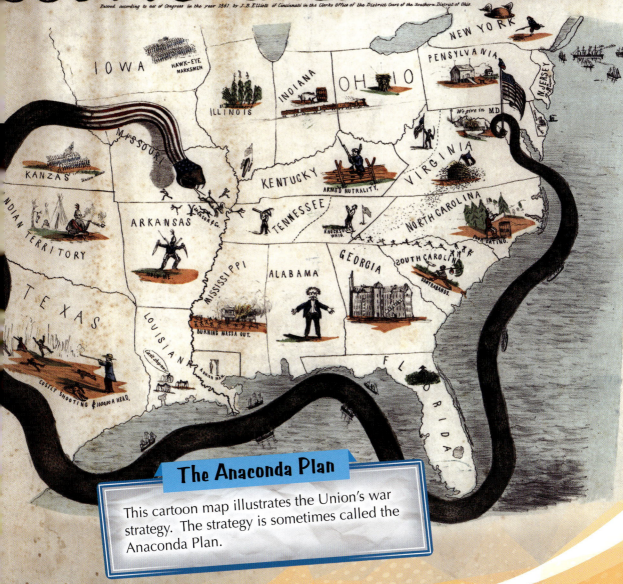

The Anaconda Plan

This cartoon map illustrates the Union's war strategy. The strategy is sometimes called the Anaconda Plan.

The Battle of Fort Brooke

On October 16, 1863, two Union ships attacked Fort Brooke. They wanted to distract the troops there. While the people at the fort were fighting, a second group marched 14 miles (22.5 kilometers) to the Hillsborough River. Their task was to destroy the blockade-runners that were there. There, they found and burned the two boats. The crews fled. On their march back, the Union force was surprised by troops from the fort. They fought briefly before making it to the ships. The Union lost 16 men. The Southern loss is unknown.

1894 depiction of the Battle of Olustee

The Battle of Olustee

The Battle of Olustee was the largest battle fought in the state during the war. On February 20, 1864, troops fought in the pinewoods near the Olustee railroad station. The Union general, Seymour, wanted to destroy the railroad bridge to cut off Southern supply lines. The Confederate general, Finnegan, started with only 500 Southern troops, but soon another 5,000 arrived. Seymour knew he had met his match after the fight raged all day. He and his men withdrew. In the end, more than 200 Union soldiers were killed and 1,152 were wounded. The South lost 93 lives and 847 were wounded.

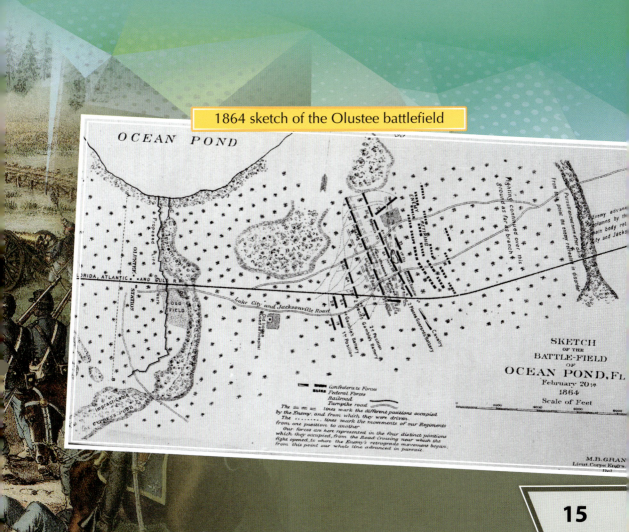

1864 sketch of the Olustee battlefield

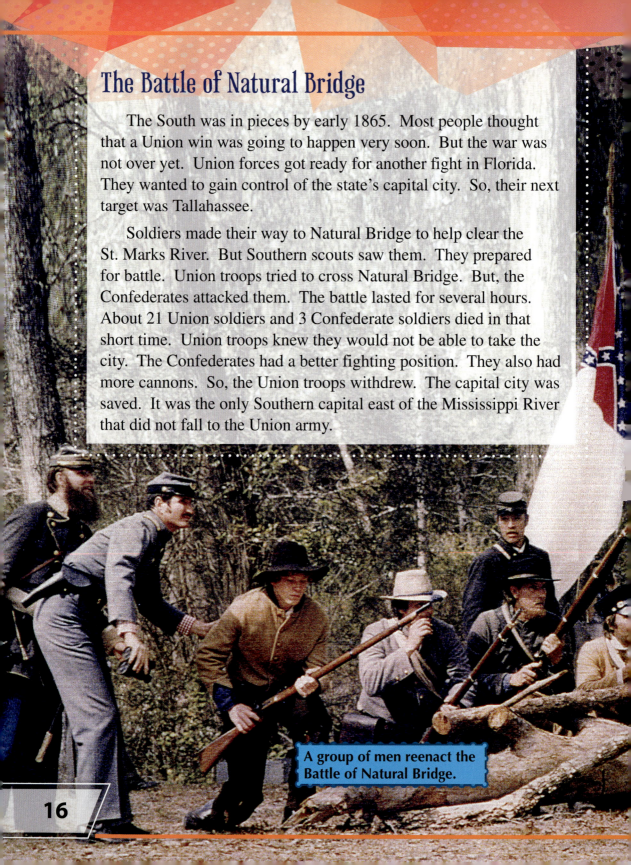

The Battle of Natural Bridge

The South was in pieces by early 1865. Most people thought that a Union win was going to happen very soon. But the war was not over yet. Union forces got ready for another fight in Florida. They wanted to gain control of the state's capital city. So, their next target was Tallahassee.

Soldiers made their way to Natural Bridge to help clear the St. Marks River. But Southern scouts saw them. They prepared for battle. Union troops tried to cross Natural Bridge. But, the Confederates attacked them. The battle lasted for several hours. About 21 Union soldiers and 3 Confederate soldiers died in that short time. Union troops knew they would not be able to take the city. The Confederates had a better fighting position. They also had more cannons. So, the Union troops withdrew. The capital city was saved. It was the only Southern capital east of the Mississippi River that did not fall to the Union army.

A group of men reenact the Battle of Natural Bridge.

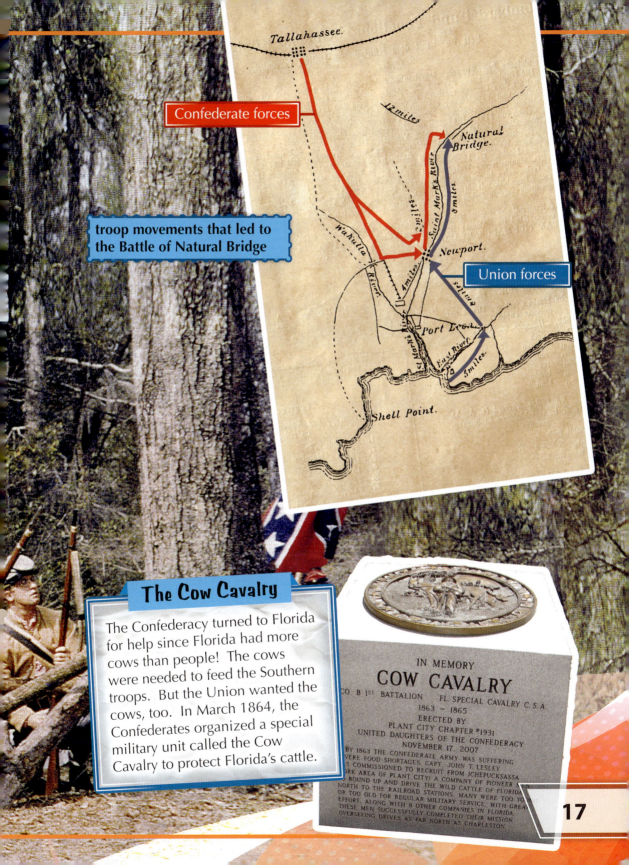

troop movements that led to the Battle of Natural Bridge

The Cow Cavalry

The Confederacy turned to Florida for help since Florida had more cows than people! The cows were needed to feed the Southern troops. But the Union wanted the cows, too. In March 1864, the Confederates organized a special military unit called the Cow Cavalry to protect Florida's cattle.

Victory!

Confederate troops in Florida were able to save their capital. They kept making salt. They sent cattle to feed the army. They protected their supply lines. But the South did not win the war. The last battle was fought four long years after the war started. Robert E. Lee surrendered the Army of Northern Virginia on April 9, 1865. The long and bloody war had been hard on everyone. Hundreds of thousands were dead. Cities were burned. Farmlands were destroyed.

Florida officially surrendered on May 10, 1865. Fifteen thousand Florida men had fought in the war. The Union victory was an important turning point for the nation. It was a turning point for Florida, as well.

Death of the President

On April 14, 1865, Lincoln and his wife Mary went to Ford's Theatre. As he sat watching the play, an assassin shot him in the head. Lincoln died the next morning. Not even a week had passed since the war had come to an end.

Robert E. Lee surrenders to Ulysses S. Grant.

Reconstruction

Reactions differed as news about the war's end spread across Florida. Many were glad. Others were angry. The war had been a great struggle. But the next step was just as hard. Now, the country had to be rebuilt. This period came to be known as the **Reconstruction** era. There had been few battles in Florida. There was not much that had been destroyed. This was not true for other Southern states. Florida was once again asked to help. Trees were plentiful in the state. Trees provided **lumber**. Lumber was needed to rebuild. Soon, the state's ports were busy shipping lumber to Florida's neighbors.

Freed slaves board a ship to move north.

Florida needed another type of rebuilding. The state's old economy was based on the plantation system. But now, slavery had ended. The plantation system could no longer function as it had in the past.

Before the war, nearly half of the state's population had been slaves. They were now free. Florida faced a great challenge. Newly freed slaves needed a place to live. They wanted an education. They wanted paying jobs. The freed slaves needed to find their place in a new Florida.

Former slaves learn to run a printing press in 1870.

The Freedmen's Bureau

In 1865, the U.S. Congress created the **Freedmen's** Bureau (BYOOR-oh). The purpose of the Bureau was to provide food, housing, and medical aid to former slaves. It also helped establish schools. In Florida, Colonel Thomas W. Osborn was responsible for overseeing the work of the Bureau.

Colonel Thomas W. Osborn

Slowly Rebuilding

Many people in the South hoped life would get back to normal after the war. But so much had changed. The families who owned plantations had very little money. But they did have land. However, landowners needed workers to do jobs that slaves used to do. Former slaves needed a place to live and a way to make money.

Landowners formed a new system. It was called **sharecropping**. Freedmen rented small plots of land from the landowners. The land was theirs to live on and cultivate. As payment, they gave part of the crops to the landowner each year. They also had to pay for tools and supplies. Freedmen owed more money than they were paid for the remaining crops.

Most sharecroppers stayed in **debt** their entire lives. Many former slaves ended up living and working on the very same lands where they had worked as slaves. Sadly, their lives were not much different than before.

sharecroppers

Black Codes

Many people in Southern states still did not think of former slaves as their equals. New laws after the Civil War kept black voters from casting ballots. The laws also forced black workers to sign yearly labor contracts. These laws were called black codes.

A freedman's services are sold to the highest bidder when he doesn't have money to pay a fine.

Rebuilding the Railroad

Florida was lucky. Its cities were still standing. The state was able to recoup quicker than other states. But, the railroads had suffered. They had been used to ship war supplies. Union forces destroyed them in the last days of the war.

After the war, people started to visit Florida. They enjoyed the mild climate. Some wanted to build winter homes there. Others wanted to move there. Some came to start new businesses. For Florida to grow, railroads had to be rebuilt. But the state had little money.

The Jupiter and Lake Worth Railroad ran 7.5 mi. (12 km) between Jupiter Inlet and Juno.

Northern businessmen had profited during the war. They took on the challenge of rebuilding Florida's railroads. Their vision was to make the state a place for tourists. Some wanted to expand trade. For this, they needed to expand Florida's railroad. By 1900, Florida had over 3,000 miles of railroad. More people could travel to the state. Many came to stay. The railroad **boom** was just beginning. The railroads helped the state move forward after the war.

David Yulee

David Yulee is remembered as the Father of Florida's Railroads. He created the Florida Railroad company in 1853. He was the first businessman in the South to use land grants, or gifts of land, to develop railroad systems in Florida. The city of Yulee was named in his honor.

Looking to the Future

The slave system of the Old South was no more. The nation reunited. But, it would take time for the wounds of war to heal. Over three thousand **homesteads** were given to freedmen. They could farm the land for themselves. This was more than any other Southern state offered. In later years, many states repealed the laws that allowed freedmen to own land.

New schools were opened across the state. Some black politicians were elected to state and national offices. But these changes did not do much for the people of the state. Florida's economy was still based on agriculture. It would be for many years to come. Farmers needed laborers. Sharecropping was a lot like slavery. The workers were still dependent laborers. Their lives were hard. They worked all the time and had little money. They could barely afford to live.

The Civil War brought a key change to Florida. There was a new foundation for equality. But, it would take more time. One hundred years after the war, people would find themselves fighting for equality once again.

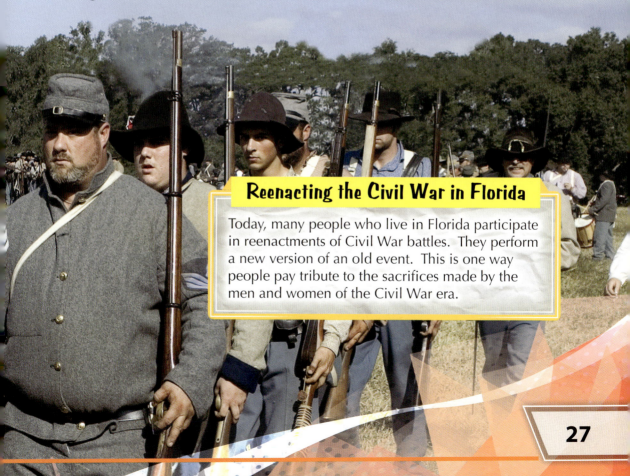

Reenacting the Civil War in Florida

Today, many people who live in Florida participate in reenactments of Civil War battles. They perform a new version of an old event. This is one way people pay tribute to the sacrifices made by the men and women of the Civil War era.

Author It!

The letters that soldiers write to family and friends tell us much about war. Read some Civil War letters. You can find many online.

Now, pretend that you are a soldier stationed at one of Florida's forts. You may choose to be a Confederate or a Union soldier. Write a letter home to your family. Tell them about your daily life at the fort during war time.

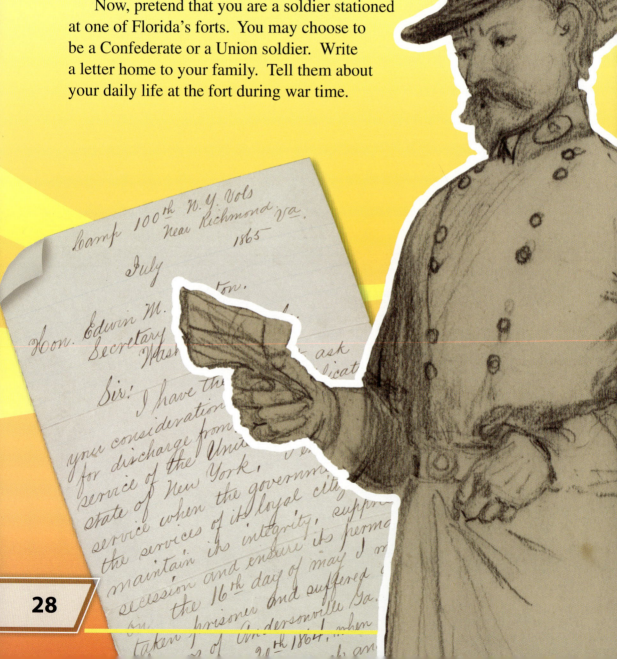

Glossary

blockade—an act of war in which ships are used to stop people and supplies from entering or leaving a country

blockade-runners—vessels or ships that attempt to get past a blockade

boom—a period of growth, progress, or sudden expansion

Confederates—people who supported the South in the Civil War; comes from the name of the country formed by the states that seceded, the Confederate States of America

debt—an amount of money owed to someone

drafted—a system in which people are forced to join the armed forces of a country

freedmen—former slaves who have been freed

homesteads—land people acquired from the government by farming and living on it

lumber—cut wood used for building

outlaw—make something against the law

plantation—a large farm that produces crops for money

Reconstruction—the years after the Civil War when the country reformed

reunite—to bring together again after a period of separation

secede—to formally separate from a nation or state

sharecropping—a system where farmers work on the owner's land for food and shelter

strategy—a careful plan to achieve a goal

surrender—to agree to stop fighting because victory is unattainable

Union—term used to describe the United States of America; also the name given to the Northern army during the Civil War

Index

Anaconda Plan, 13, 32

black codes, 23

Broward, Helen, 7

Confederate States of America, 8

Cow Cavalry, 17

Fort Brooke, Battle of, 14

Fort Pickens, 8

Fort Sumter, 9

Freedmen's Bureau, 21

Lee, Robert E., 18–19

Lincoln, Abraham, 4, 6, 9, 18

Natural Bridge, Battle of, 16–17

Olustee, Battle of, 14–15

Osborn, Thomas W., 21

Pensacola Bay, 8

reenactments, 27

Santa Rosa Island, 8

Yulee, David, 25

Your Turn!

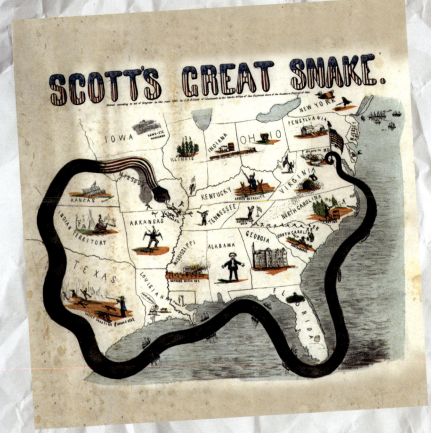

Plan of Attack

In war, both sides plan their strategies carefully. They plan where, when, and how to attack. Create a minibattlefield with toy soldiers or other small objects. Sketch out a plan for your attack. Have a friend do the same. Then, compare plans to see who would have won.